303 of the World's Worst Predictions

By WAYNE COFFEY

COMMUNICATIONS, INC.
New York

ACKNOWLEDGMENTS

Special thanks are due Carl Waldman, for his valuable research and writing contributions, and to Frank Coffey, who bolstered his brother when he needed bolstering and supplied an appropriately wicked hand with the headlines.

DEDICATION

For my family: Mom, Allison and Frank; Vic and Chris, who are like family; and D. W., who is like nobody else.

Library of Congress Cataloging in Publication Data

Coffey, Wayne
 303 of the world's worst predictions.

 1. Quotations, English.   3. Forecasting—Miscellanea.
I. Title.   II. Title: Three hundred three of the world's worst predictions.
III. Title: Three hundred and three of the world's worst predictions.
PN6083.C57   1983   081   83-9128
ISBN 0-943392-19-5 (pbk.)

Written by Wayne R. Coffey
All illustrations by Steven DuQuette

Distributed in Canada by Prentice-Hall Canada, Inc.,
1870 Birchmont Road, Scarborough, Ontario M1P 2J7

Printed in the United States of America

First Edition: September 1983

1   2   3   4   5   6   7   8   9   10

TABLE OF CONTENTS

INTRODUCTION

"The prophesying business," wrote H. L. Mencken, "is fatal to everyone save the man of absolute genius." This book offers ample evidence of how few absolute geniuses there are.

The evidence comes from many different domains and many different people. You may not have thought Aristotle, Billy Martin and Winston Churchill have a whole lot in common, but there is at least this much: they've all made pretty bad predictions. So have a lot of other people (I once said, "I'll never live in New York City," and guess where I'm parked right now?). The only difference is that the people here got caught.

Working on this book has taught me two valuable lessons. One, what a great cure for anything it is to spend all of one's time focusing on other people's mistakes. And two, that probably 90 percent of what's passed off as gospel today will end up in a book like this tomorrow.

Read on. You may never feel smarter.

—Wayne Coffey

1
MISLEADERS
Politics/Government

Do send us a postcard

"The beauties of the Crimea, which we shall make accessible by means of an autobahn—for us Germans, that will be our Riviera."

Adolf Hitler (1941)

Quite contrary, Mary

"McGovern will beat Nixon in a landslide."

Mary McGrory, newspaper columnist (October 22, 1972)

For whom the Liberty Bell tolls

"Democracy will be dead by 1950."

John Langdon-Davies, A Short History of the Future (1936)

On to the galaxy

"We are winning international respect."

Adolph Hitler (1934)

Mayo or mustard with that?

"If Jimmy Carter gets the Democratic nomination, I'll eat a big bowl of guano."

Victor H. Rosenthal, college student (1976)

Imagine if his program had been a failure

"The Republican Party goes into the contest with its best contender, under conditions favorable to success. . . Mr. Hoover's knowledge and experience are factors of strength, and the remarkable success of his program of rehabilitation is in his favor. . ."

A Washington Post editorial (1932)

Speak softly, and hope nobody hears you

"I would not accept."

Theodore Roosevelt, replying to the suggestion that he run as Vice-President on the McKinley ticket (1900)

Is there a wheelbarrow handy?

"The biggest lot of crap I've ever heard in my life."

Robert Mardian, of President Nixon's Committee to Reelect the President, responding to allegations of his involvement in the Watergate break-in

Easy for you to say, Chubs

"Up until recent times the production of food has been the prime struggle of man. That war is won."

> Winston Churchill, addressing the subject, "Fifty Years Hence" (1932)

But I do like the parchment it's written on

"Your Constitution is all sail and no anchor . . ."

> Thomas Babington Macauley, British writer and statesman (1857)

Ledger-demaine

"There is absolutely no question about the city's ability to repay all of its debts on time."

> Abe Beame, Mayor of New York City (1975)

I've always been the trusting type

"Stalin . . . doesn't want anything but security for his country, and I think that if I give him everything I possibly can and ask nothing from him in return, noblese oblige, he won't try to annex anything and will work with me for a world democracy and peace."

> Franklin Delano Roosevelt, as reported by William C. Bullitt (1948)

Trust me

"This is a dream I've always looked forward to—a place where I can be happy going no further politically."

> U.S. Senator Al D'Amato after being elected town supervisor of Hempstead in 1978, two years before making a successful run for the Senate

Tell it to the Ayatollah

"Iran will be an island of stability in the Third World sea of change."

> Institute for the Future, think tank (1973)

We're out of Sherwin-Williams

"There can be no whitewash at the White House."

> President Richard Nixon (1973)

Nothing a good missile crisis can't cure

"Never in the past has there been any place on the globe where the vital interests of American and Russian people have clashed or even been antagonistic . . . and there is no objective reason to suppose there should be now or in the future ever such a place."

> Dean Acheson, Secretary of State under President Harry Truman

Bolshit

"What are the Bolsheviki? They are the representatives of the most democratic government in Europe . . . Let us recognize the truest democracy in Europe, the truest democracy in the world today."

> Publisher William Randolph Hearst (1918)

But I wouldn't rule out slinking

"I want you to know that I have no intention whatever of ever walking away from the job that the American people elected me to do for the people of the United States."

> President Richard Nixon (January 1974)

Get rid of the Blum

"Better Hitler than Blum."

> Slogan by French conservatives in the 1930s, when Leon Blum, a Socialist, was the nation's premier

Why don't we vote on it?

"For the tasks of the next century, the methods of popular representation and parliaments are the most inappropriate imaginable."

> Friedrich Nietzsche, German philosopher (1885)

Vodka's a close second

"Gaiety is the most outstanding feature of the Soviet Union."

Joseph Stalin (1935)

Nobody told Mahatma

"British rule in India will endure. By 2030, whatever means of self-government India has achieved, she will still remain a loyal and integral part of the British Empire.

Earl of Birkenwood, British politician (1930)

Say it were so, Joe

"The past was sad, and the future looks dark and gloomy; all chances and hopes have quite disappeared."

Nazi propagandist Joseph Goebbels, on the state of the Nazi Party in 1932

So what's a little repression here and there?

"Comrades, we are building not a land of idlers where rivers flow with milk and honey, but the most organized and most industrious society in human history. And the people living in that society will be the most industrious, conscientious, organized, politically conscious group in history."

Leonid Brezhnev (1972)

Ask me again in forty-eight hours

"It's too early for a Polish Pope."

> Pope John Paul II, two days before his ascendancy to the Papacy

Bonzo on the bread line

"I see our economic program as the best hope we've got for solving the unemployment problem."

> President Ronald Reagan (1981)

Whiteout

"We have the happiest Africans in the world."

> Ian Smith, Rhodesian Prime Minister (1971)

"There are going to be no dramatic changes in Rhodesia."

> Ian Smith (1975)

"I don't believe in black majority rule ever in Rhodesia, not in a thousand years."

> Ian Smith (1976)

At least that's what my palm reader tells me

"This election could well be a real cliffhanger. . ."

> George Gallup, pollster, on the 1980 presidential election

Voodoo can be fun

". . . by 1983 my program can bring about a balanced budget and begin to bring in surpluses so that we can have additional tax cuts beyond those we have already suggested."

President Ronald Reagan (1981)

Take 'em

"A hundred to one."

Jimmy "The Greek" Snyder, making the odds for President Richard Nixon leaving office before his term expired

All we have to do is hit Free Parking

"The national debt will be paid."

L. N. Boyd, editor of The Fairmont (West Virginia) Gazette, offering a prediction for 1967 (1867)

A long boat

"We shall reach the helm within five years."

Sir Oswald Mosley, a leader of the Fascist Party in England (1938)

False profit

"We are moving to the victory of communism."

Nikita Khrushchev (1955)

Dewey or don't he?

"Dewey is sure to be elected. I predict he will be a first-rate President."

> Drew Pearson, syndicated news-paper columnist (October 14, 1948)

"Dewey is in, of course."

> Business Week (October 30, 1948)

"Dewey is going to be the next President, and you might as well get used to him."

> New Republic (October 22, 1948)

We must have gotten our second wind

"The murderous liberal-capitalist era is now breathing its last. Adolf Hitler and his National Socialist idea for the redemption of people will conquer for the weal of that people, and will enjoy a long peace."

> Yeinrich Lohse, Living Age magazine, (c. 1935)

That's probably why I'm unemployed today

"I think that liberalism is going to be more, rather than less, relevant in the coming years."

> Former U.S. Senator George McGovern of South Dakota (1978)

Anyone for a sense of truth?

"What we have to give our people, our young people particularly, is a sense of excitement, a sense of challenge, a sense of destiny, and only when they have that are they going to have any sense of satisfaction. That is really our job."

President Richard Nixon, looking toward the 1970s (1969)

Makes a nice speech, though

"This man Churchill is the enemy of the British Empire ... This man Churchill is a warmonger. He is turning the thoughts of the British Empire to war. He must be stopped."

Lord Beaverbrook, as quoted by Patrick Campbell (1939)

U said it

"I do not wish to seem overdramatic but I can only conclude from the information that is available to me as Secretary-General that the members of the United Nations have perhaps ten years left in which to subordinate their ancient quarrels and launch a global partnership to curb the arms race, to improve the human environment, to defuse the population explosion, and to supply the required momentum to development efforts. If such a global partnership is not formed within the next decade, then I very much fear that the problems I have mentioned will have reached such staggering proportions that they will be beyond our capacity to control."

U Thant, former Secretary-General of the United Nations (1969)

Three Reichs and you're out

"I have no war aims against Great Britain and France."

Adolf Hitler (1939)

"Soldiers of the West Front: The battle which is beginning today will decide the fate of the German nation for the next thousand years."

Adolf Hitler (1940)

"To this city of Paris, where the flag of Germany shall fly for a thousand years."

General Feldmarschall Hugo Sperrle, just days before the liberation of Paris by Allied troops, offering a toast

Neville in dreamland

"For the second time in our history, a British Prime Minister has returned from Germany bringing peace with honor. I believe it is a peace for our time . . . Go home and get a nice quiet sleep."

British Prime Minister Neville Chamberlain (1938)

One for two

"I'll never run again. Politics is a filthy business."

Ed Koch, Mayor of New York City, after losing in an assembly primary early in his career (1962)

Hugh don't say?

"Nobody is paying any attention to what you're writing."

> U.S. Senator Hugh Scott of Pennsylvania, commenting at a press conference to Carl Bernstein and Bob Woodward, who were probing into the Watergate scandal in <u>The Washington Post</u>

Only mastermind it

"There is no place in our campaign or in the electoral process for this type of activity, and we will not permit or condone it."

> John Mitchell, head of the Committee to Reelect the President (CREEP), after the Watergate break-in (1972)

Il Dunce

Fascism is a religion; the twentieth century will be known in history as the century of Fascism."

> Benito Mussolini, commenting in the wake of Hitler's accession to power

Let's toast shortsightedness

"I will never see the day when the Eighteenth Amendment (Prohibition) is out of the Constitution of the U.S."

> U.S. Senator William Borah (1929)

Good thing funerals are deductible

"Capitalism is dying, and its extremities are already decomposing. The blotches upon the surface show that the blood no longer circulates. The time is near when the cadaver will have to be removed and the atmosphere purified."

> Eugene V. Debs, American labor leader (1904)

What, me manipulative?

"We have finished with the prewar policy of colonies and trade, and are going over to the land policy of the future. When we talk of acquiring new lands in Europe we think first of Russia and her border states . . . For such a policy there is only one possible ally—England."

> Adolf Hitler, Mein Kampf

How 'bout just bolting?

"The Shah cannot, will not, and is legally incapable of abdicating."

> Iranian ambassador Ardeshir Zahedi (1979)

And I'll be reelected in 1932 . . .

". . . Prosperity is right around the corner."

> President Herbert Hoover on the state of the union (1930)

Stamp out inflation

"Letter postage will be one cent instead of three."

L. N. Boyd, editor of The Fairmont
(West Virginia) Gazette, looking
toward 1967 (1867)

Nice theory, anyway

"In the twentieth century, there will be an extraordinary nation. This nation will be illustrious, thoughtful, pacific, cordial to the rest of mankind . . . The capital of this nation will be Paris, but its country will not be France. In the twentieth century, its country will be called Europe, and in after centuries, as it still and ever develops, it will be called mankind."

Victor Hugo, French writer (1842)

2
ARE WE THERE YET?

Transportation

Besides, I've always loved the smell of manure

"Nothing has come along that can beat the horse and buggy."

> Chauncey Depew, U.S. businessman, on why he was against investing in Henry Ford's nascent company

Soar loser

"Man won't fly for a thousand years."

> Wilbur Wright, to brother Orville after a disappointing flying experiment (1901)

How 'bout the locomotives being on time?

"What can be more palpably absurd than the prospect held out of locomotives traveling twice as fast as stagecoaches?"

> The Quarterly Review (1825)

A steam of invective

"What, sir? You would make a ship sail against the wind and currents by lighting a bonfire under her decks? I pray you excuse me. I have no time to listen to such nonsense."

> Napoleon Bonaparte to Robert Fulton, upon hearing of the latter's plans for a steam-powered engine

But what do I know? I write fairy tales

"Yes, in a thousand years, people will fly on the wings of steam through the air, over the ocean."

> Hans Christian Andersen, Danish Author (1853)

Hans told me

"In about three years commercial planes will fly from New York to California in one hour."

> Dr. Alexander Lippisch, U.S. Air Force researcher (1948)

Put it into the tank, Hank

". . . my gas-engine experiments were no more popular with the president of the company than my first mechanical leanings were with my father. It was not that my employer objected to experiments—only to experiments with a gas engine. I can still hear him say: 'Electricity yes, that's the coming thing. But gas, no.'"

> Henry Ford, My Life and Work (1922)

Choo now, vomit later

"These locomotive engines will be a terrible nuisance in consequences of the fire and smoke vomited forth by them."

> A committee of the English
> Parliament (1825)

He does well in gym, though

"That Professor Goddard with his 'chair' in Clark College and the countenancing of the Smithsonian does not know the relation of action to inaction, and of the need to have something better than a vacuum against which to react—to say that would be absurd. Of course he only seems to lack the knowledge ladled out daily in high schools . . ."

> A New York Times editorial of January 13, 1920, on Robert Goddard, who later became known as "the father of American rocketry"

But the theoretical building is going great guns

"The actual building of roads devoted to motor cars is not for the near future, in spite of many rumors to that effect."

> Harper's Weekly (1902)

It'll-never-fly Department

"Heavier-than-air flying machines are impossible."

> Lord Kelvin, engineer and physicist (c. 1890)

Save this one for rush hour

"The ordinary horseless carriage is, at present, a luxury for the wealthy; and although its price will probably fall in the near future, it will never, of course, come into as common use as the bicycle."

Literary Digest (1899)

Go for an atom?

"I have not the smallest molecule of faith in aerial navigation other than ballooning."

Lord Kelvin, engineer and physicist (c. 1890)

The little engine that couldn't

". . . any general system of conveying passengers—at a velocity exceeding ten miles per hour, or thereabouts—is extremely improbable."

Thomas Tredgold, British railroad designer (1835)

Orange you glad you were wrong?

"The possession of this Russian territory can give us neither honor, wealth, nor power, but will always be a source of weakness and expense, without any adequate return."

U.S. Congressman Orange Ferriss, on a proposal to purchase Alaska from Russia (1868)

It's all moonshine

"In all fairness to those who by training are not prepared to evaluate the fundamental difficulties of going from one planet to another, or even from the earth to the moon, it must be stated that there is not the slightest possibility of such journeys."

F. R. Moulton, American astronomer (1935)

At least we won't have to bring our own vodka

"If we continue at this leisurely pace, we will have to pass through Russian customs on the moon."

Scientist Werner von Braun, on the United States' languishing efforts in the space race (1959)

See your travel agent today

"For the tourist who really wants to get away from it all— safaris in Vietnam."

Newsweek, in an article looking ahead to 1970 (1959)

Take the long way home

"The Panama Canal is actually a thing of the past, and Nature in her works will soon obliterate all traces of French energy and money expended on the Isthmus."

Scientific American (1891)

Bad news for the body clock

"It will be only a comparatively short time before a trip from Paris to New York can be made in twenty-four minutes and a trip around the world in an hour and a half."

Robert Esnault-Pelterie, French scientist (1930)

What's the latest line on this one?

"There's even a fifty-fifty possibility that civilians will be able to fly in atomic-powered planes or travel in atomic-powered vessels by 1975."

Changing Times magazine (1961)

If you come out of your compartment, I'll come out of mine

"This foolish idea of shooting at the moon is an example of the absurd length to which vicious specialization will carry scientists working in thought-tight compartments."

A. W. Bickerton, British physicist (1926)

Can aerial meter maids be far behind?

"Businessmen will commute to work in helicopters small enough to fit easily in garages. Traffic cops will rule the skies."

William Fielding Ogburn, professor of sociology, University of Chicago (1943)

Ditch it

"All mankind has heard much of M. Lesseps and his Suez Canal . . . I have a very strong opinion that such canal will not and cannot be made."

Anthony Trollope, British novelist (1860)

But that was before hot tubs

". . . I cannot conceive of anything more ridiculous, more absurd and more affrontive to sober judgment than the cry that we are profiting by the acquisition of New Mexico and California. I hold that they are not worth a dollar."

U.S. Senator Daniel Webster (1848)

He's probably a landlord back East

". . . The vast and unmanageable extent which the accession of Louisiana will give to the United States . . . threatens, at no very distant day, the subversion of our Union."

U.S. Congressman Roger Griswold, arguing against the Louisiana Purchase (1803)

We certainly will be busy, won't we?

"Men will travel through the air more than they do, make themselves unseen (though with difficulty), reach the North Pole and the top of Mount Everest (all to no purpose), see through mountains and across continents, hear the inaudible, store sunlight and sunheat, and solve the secret of the sun."

John D. Rogers, writer, forecasting the world of 1920 (1904)

Just another big hole

"It is, of course, altogether valueless . . . Ourselves are the first, and doubtless will be the last, party of whites to visit this profitless locality. It seems intended by nature that the Colorado River shall be forever unvisited and undisturbed."

> Lieutenant Joseph Ives, Corps of Topographical Engineers, on the Grand Canyon (1861)

And (7), he's a crummy sailor

> A committee, organized to study Columbus' plan to sail west to discover a shorter route to the Indies, reporting to King Ferdinand and Queen Isabella of Spain in 1486 that the trip was impossible because

". . . (1) A voyage to Asia would require three years. (2) The Western Ocean is infinite and perhaps unnavigable. (3) If he reached the Antipodes [the land on the other side of the globe from Europe] he could not get back. (4) There are no Antipodes because the greater part of the globe is covered with water, and because Saint Augustine says so . . . (5) Of the five zones, only three are habitable. (6) So many centuries after the Creation it was unlikely that anyone could find hitherto unknown lands of any value."

This one doesn't hold much water

"I cannot imagine any condition which could cause this ship to flounder. I cannot conceive of any vital disaster happening to this vessel. Modern shipbuilding has gone beyond that."

> E. J. Smith, Captain of the Titanic

WEBSTER

TROLLOPE

Gridlock, Schmidlock

"Surface travel (in New York) will be an oddity in twenty years."

John B. McDonald, builder of New York's first subway (1903)

Right up there with death and taxes

"Aerial flight is one of that class of problems with which man will never be able to cope."

Simon Newcomb, American astronomer (1903)

Rudderly absurd

". . . even if the propeller had the power of propelling a vessel, it would be found altogether useless in practice, because the power being applied in the stern it would be absolutely impossible to make the vessel steer."

Sir William Symonds, surveyor of the British Navy (1837)

Leave the driving to us

"What about electronic highways—enabling drivers to sit back and enjoy the scenery while electronic devices guide and operate the car? You may see stretches, and some cars properly equipped to use them, by 1975."

Changing Times magazine, issuing a prediction for 1975 (1961)

The party planet

"I can tell from here . . . what the inhabitants of Venus are like; they resemble the Moors of Granada: a small, black people, burned by the sun, full of wit and fire, always in love, writing verse, fond of music, arranging festivals, dances and tournaments every day."

> Bernard de Fontenelle, French author (1686)

Plastered in Paris

"Travel will be the chief recreation of the future. An American will think nothing of spending a weekend in Argentina or the Himalayas or dining one evening in Paris and turning up at the office on time the next morning."

> Waldemar Kaempffert, American science writer (1941)

So what's all the flap about?

"If God had intended that man should fly, He would have given him wings."

> Widely attributed to George W. Melville, chief engineer of the U.S. Navy (c. 1900)

Can McDonald's be far behind?

"One or more permanent bases will have been established on the moon."

> Edward C. Welsh, former Executive Secretary, NASA, predicting for 1982

3

SOCIABULL

Sociology

How's that again?

"Thanks to the increasing efficiency of the machine, the city of the future will be completely noiseless."

Arthur Train, American lawyer and writer (1941)

Could be trouble for soul music

". . . In less than thirty years time . . . there will be only two races left of any real account in the world, two world rulers of the future, namely the Anglicans or Anglo Saxons and the Slavs."

Living Age magazine (1896)

Does anyone know how to say "bullshit" in Nepali?

"Competition with Iron Curtain education, plus the need to prepare citizens for the world of tomorrow, will leave youngsters studying Russian, Chinese, and Japanese and the other tongues of Asia and Africa. Language instruction will begin in the fourth grade."

Changing Times magazine, a forecast for 1975 (1961)

Bill Glass?

"In five years, men will be wearing suits and sportswear made out of glass-waterproof, fireproof, washable glass."

Guy Marino, Jr., fashion designer (1948)

You go that way, I'll go this way

"Crime detection will be highly scientific, deadly sure."

William Fielding Ogburn, professor of sociology, University of Chicago, projecting the world of 1970 (1943)

You're just saying that to make us feel better

"My figures coincide in fixing 1950 as the year when the world must go to smash."

Henry Adams, American historian (1903)

He must've been from the Sun Belt

"We are on the eve of the most eventful period of mankind. Migration of millions from north to south will soon take place, and new nations and empires will be founded by them, superior in every respect to any known in history."

J. A. Etzler, The Paradise Within the Reach of All Men (1836)

Cages'll be more like it

"By 1975 parents will have ceased to bring up their children in private family units."

John Langdon-Davies, A Short History of The Future (1936)

Dad, can I have the chopper tonight?

"The family helicopter will be as attainable as the family convertible is today."

Life magazine, a forecast for 1980 (1970)

The union'll push for two

"By 1960 work will be limited to three hours a day."

John Langdon-Davies, A Short History of the Future (1936)

One for four isn't too bad

"In the twentieth century war will be dead, the scaffold will be dead, animosity will be dead, but man will live."

Victor Hugo, French writer (1842)

What about a drought?

". . . we need never fear for a fuel oil famine."

Rogert W. Babson, scientist (1928)

But I wish I did

"I do not hesitate to forecast that atomic batteries will be commonplace long before 1980."

> David Sarnoff, former chairman of RCA (1955)

Life without sects

"There will be no Methodists and Prebyterians or Baptists. All will be one denomination."

> L. N. Boyd, editor of the Fairmont (West Virginia) Gazette, offering a prediction for 1967 (1867)

Thought we'd forget?

"Ten years from now, faculties will include Biochemical therapists/pharmacists, whose services increase as biochemical therapy and memory-improvement chemicals are introduced more widely."

> Harold and June Shane, professors of education, University of Indiana, on education in 1980 (1969)

Socket to me

"Electricity will cost less than one tenth of a cent per kilowatt hour."

> Dr. R. M. Langer, California Institute of Technology (1941)

But will they get things whiter than white?

"Ultrasonic sound waves will wash dishes and clothes."

Changing Times magazine, forecasting the world of 1975 (1961)

Darker tonight, lighter tomorrow

"Regular and reliable weather forecasts are given fourteen days in advance for areas as small as one hundred square miles."

Paul Dickson, citing predictions for 1980 made by think tanks (1979)

Now stop screwing off and get back to the rock pile

"It is safe to say that by 1970, all backbreaking work will be done by machine power. And I mean all. Men will work only six hours a day, four days a week."

William Fielding Ogburn, professor of sociology, University of Chicago (1943)

So what if they can't read

"In the late 1970s or early 1980s, it is not unlikely that students will graduate from high school with knowledge and social insight equal to or superior to that of the person who earned a bachelor's degree in the 1960s."

Harold and June Shane, professors of education, University of Indiana, on education in 1980 (1969)

Anybody hungry?

"To kill a man will be considered as disgusting as we in this day consider it disgusting to eat one."

> Andrew Carnegie, on the purging of violence in the twentieth century (1901)

In the meantime, fork over your money

"Crime will be considered a disease after 1985 and will cease to exist by A.D. 2000."

> John Langdon-Davies, <u>A Short History of the Future</u> (1936)

Bad news for real estate brokers

"The population of the earth decreases every day, and if this continues, in another ten centuries the earth will be nothing but a desert."

> Montesquieu, French philosopher (1743)

Reading and rioting

"I thank God there are no free schools, nor printing, and hope we shall not have them these hundred years; for learning has brought disobedience and heresay and sects into the world, and printing has divulged them and libels against the ...."

> Sir William Berkeley, royal governor of Virginia (1670)

Where there's a bill there's a way

"The doctor and dentist shortage will become a major public concern."

Changing Times magazine, a forecast for 1975 (1961)

Bad news for the glee club

"The day of individual happiness has passed."

Adolf Hitler (1934)

Immaculate Conception

"... Cities will become sanitary—no dirt, dust or smoke will be possible. The streets will be beautifully clean."

Charles Steinmetz, American electrical engineer, foreseeing an electrical world (1915)

Plugging into paradise

"Watt and the individualistic steam engine gave us tenements, jungles of stone and steel, forests of chimneys, high rents, clogged street cars and subways, slums, diseases unknown among savages. And the electrical engineers of today? Thousands of small towns with plenty of garden space, low rents, breathing space, open-air sports for all, servantless houses in which electricity is the maid of all work, health and a finer outlook on life."

Waldemar Kaempffert, American science writer (1929)

What, me hurry?

"We shall probably find the public taste changing, so that many people will prefer to travel from place to place more slowly than at present."

Cleveland Moffett, American writer, on life after automobiles have become commonplace (1900)

Gunpoint is much more convenient anyway

"Picketing as a means of shaking down employers will be barred."

U.S. News and World Report discussing a law being considered by Congress (1959)

Neighbor au gratin

"When we get piled upon one another in large cities, we shall become as corrupt as in Europe, and go to eating one another as they do there."

Thomas Jefferson (1787)

That's rebatable

"The three-, four- and five-car family is to grow in number in the decade ahead."

U.S. News and World Report, looking into the world of the 1970s (1969)

Pampers 101

"... Education will assume a formal responsibility for children when they reach the age of two."

Harold and June Shane, professors of education, on future trends (1969)

Now let's work on affordable

"Abundant new raw materials will (by 1960) make food, clothing, and other necessities universally obtainable."

John Langdon-Davies, A Short History of the Future (1936)

The Pig Apple

"By the year 1900, Brooklyn undoubtedly will be the city, and Manhattan will be the suburb. Brooklyn has room to grow; Manhattan has not. The New Yorker uptown on 35th Street already finds it a tedious and annoying job to commute to his business downtown and home again. Can you imagine him fighting his way all the way up to the pig farms on 100th Street forty years hence?"

George Templeton Strong, American lawyer and diarist (1865)

Got anything with a pantry and 2½ baths?

"The day may come when enterprising citizens will trade their houses in every so often against a new model."

Arthur Train, American lawyer and writer (1941)

But think how easy parking'll be

"The time will come when the great city of New York will be left without inhabitants."

> Orson Pratt, a Mormon prophecy from The Journal of Discourses (c. 1840)

Such a bloody fun way to pass an afternoon

"Executions are so much a part of British history that it is almost impossible for many excellent people to think of the future without them."

> Viscount Templewood, In the Shadow of the Gallows (1951)

Take this with a grain of salt

"It is abundantly clear that by 1975 routine desalinization of sea water will be indispensable to an adequate water supply."

> Changing Times magazine (1961)

Think how many more dumb predictions we'll be able to make

"A much shorter work week will no doubt prevail in 1980, and another ten or fifteen years will have been added to the average life span."

> David Sarnoff, former chairman of RCA, forecasting for 1980 (1955)

Who's gonna break it to the cows?

"Don't get excited until you see it, but there's a chance you'll buy your week's supply of fresh milk at the grocery store one of these days—in a package of milk cubes. The cubes, now being experimented with, are dry, wrapped and can be kept several weeks in your refrigerator. Drop a cube in a glass of water and there's milk—fresh, whole milk again without that "condensed" taste of milk from cans."

Good Housekeeping (1943)

Whisky proposition

"Instead of just being aged in tar wood, whisky of the future can be made of it."

Dr. Robert S. Aries, Brooklyn Polytechnic Institute (1948)

A pack a day keeps the doctor away

"The power of tobacco to sustain the system, to keep up nutrition, to maintain and increase the weight, to brace against severe exertion, and to replace ordinary food, is a matter of daily and hourly demonstration."

George Black, The Doctor at Home, (c. 1898)

A bad guy to tick off

"God is going to punish the world, and very soon."

Sister Lucy, Catholic missionary (1959)

Last call

"... The direct and indirect wastefulness of alcohol will make it impossible for beverages containing it to be tolerated."

> T. Baron Russell, <u>A Hundred Years Hence</u> (1905)

Good news for us mental midgets

"Grade cards likewise are destined to disappear."

> Harold and June Shane, professors of education, University of Indiana, forecasting for 1980 (1969)

4
TRIPPING OVER THE BOTTOM LINE
Business/Economics

See your loan shark for further details

"Interest rates will slide until midyear at least, giving a lift to the depressed auto and housing industries."

U.S. News and World Report
(January 1982)

Somebody's got to do the dirty work

' "The alarming development and aggressiveness of great capitalists and corporations, unless checked, will inevitably lead to the pauperization and hopeless degradation of the toiling masses."

Constitution of the Knights of Labor,
United States (c. 1869)

The Hazards of Economic Forecasting (Part I)

"There will be an abundance of jobs and a sharp rise in buying power."

U.S. News and World Report, forecasting the 1970s (1969)

The Hazards of Economic Forecasting (Part II)

"Many people will be realizing income half again as big as now, working fewer hours to attain it."

U.S. News and World Report (1969)

Anyone for lemons?

". . . the President's program will begin to bear fruit even before it is enacted."

Donald Regan, U.S. Secretary of the Treasury, on President Reagan's economic plan (1981)

For more, see his new book (it's only $69.95)

"In all likelihood, world inflation is over."

Managing Director, International Monetary Fund (1959)

So what if I just sold all my stocks

"[The] . . . fundamental business of the country . . . is on a sound and prosperous basis."

President Herbert Hoover (Black Friday 1929)

Boom-erang

"Foreseen is a full-employment economy, with only 3.5 percent jobless, inflation in the neighborhood of 3 percent per year. That, in effect, is the price to be paid for the boom times of the '70s."

U.S. News and World Report, forecasting the 1970s (1969)

The buck plops here

"Inflation will shrink the dollar another 25 percent."

Changing Times magazine, forecasting the world of 1975 (1961)

Gimme shelter

"The avoidance of taxes is the only intellectual pursuit that still carries any reward."

John Maynard Keynes (1883-1946), English economist

They paid us to say this

"The trade of advertising is now so near to perfection that it is not easy to propose any improvement."

The Idler, an English newspaper (1759)

5
STRAY BULLETS

War and the Military

At last, guilt-free bombing

"The robot plane with a selenium eye will become the great future weapon."

Edwin L. Rice, aircraft manufacturer (1938)

How's this for vintage British understatement?

"Atomic energy might be as good as our present-day explosives, but it is unlikely to produce anything very much more dangerous."

Winston Churchill (1939)

Take a bow

". . . The bow is a simple weapon, firearms are very complicated things which get out of order in many ways. . . a very heavy weapon and tires out soldiers on the march. Whereas also a bowman can let off six aimed shots a minute, a musketeer can discharge but one in two minutes."

Colonel Sir John Smyth, advising the British Privy Council not to forsake the bow for the musket (1591)

Chink in the armor

"I will not live to see what you will witness if you live your ordinary life. That will be the conquest of China by Japan, and when that is done, the conquest of all the island possessions from north to south."

Admiral John Dewey (1942)

Let's flip a coin and skip the war

"England and America will one day have a war with one another which will be waged with the greatest hatred imaginable. One of the two countries will have to disappear."

Adolf Hitler, Table Talk (1941)

Sure glad we said "seems"

"The one trend that seems inevitable during the '60s is a continuing reduction in armed-forces manpower, as weapons become increasingly potent and expensive. Another is the consolidation of the Army, Navy, Air Force and Marines."

Newsweek (1959)

Loose lips

"As far as sinking a ship with a bomb is concerned, you just can't do it."

U.S. Navy Rear Admiral Clark Woodward (1939)

Should be over any decade now

"The war in Vietnam is going well and will succeed."

> Robert McNamara, U.S. Secretary of Defense (1963)

Depends on whether it's behind you or in front of you

"A grossly overrated weapon."

> British Field Marshal Haig, offering his opinion of the newly invented machine gun, around the time of World War I

. . . And then stop making predictions

"Hitler is already defeated. Russia has defeated him, not the British Army or Navy. His aggression against his smaller and weaker neighbors has been effectively checked . . . Clearly the best thing to do is to stop the war by a truce."

> J. A. Salter, member of Parliament, at the beginning of World War II

Go for three?

"Major fighting in Vietnam will peter out about 1967."

"Lyndon Johnson will be reelected in 1968."

> Ithiel de Sola Pool, Massachusetts Institute of Technology political scientist (1965)

Reach for the sky, partner

> "[Before] the 20th century closes, the earth will be purged of its foulest shame, the killing of men in battle under the name of war."

> Andrew Carnegie (1901)

A promise that will live in infamy

> "And while I am talking to you mothers and fathers, I give you more assurance; I have said this before, but I shall say it again and again and again: Your boys are not going to be sent into any foreign wars."

> President Franklin D. Roosevelt (1940)

How's the mileage?

> "In a few years, the U.S. Air Force's B-70 bomber will be operational. The bat-shaped plane will swoosh through the air at Mach 3—three times the speed of sound, or about 2,000 miles per hour."

> Changing Times magazine (1961)

Look out for the second flurry, though

> "In the event of [nuclear] war, after the first flurry of activity . . . this ship will still be there."

> Captain Arlington F. Campbell, on the Trident submarine (1981)

Until the next one

"It [the Sudetenland] is the last territorial claim that I have to make in Europe."

Adolf Hitler (1938)

Give or take 990

"By this revolution the German way of life is definitely settled for the next thousand years."

Adolf Hitler (1934)

Tanks just the same

"The idea that cavalry will be replaced by these iron coaches is absurd. It is little short of treasonous."

British military official to Field Marshal Haig, after witnessing a tank demonstration (1916)

To air is human

"The day of the battleship has not passed, and it is highly unlikely that an airplane, or fleet of them, could ever success-fully sink a fleet of navy vessels under battle conditions."

Franklin D. Roosevelt, Assistant Secretary of the Navy (1922)

Yellow around the edges

"The Japanese are occupying all the islands, one after another. They will get hold of Australia, too. The White Race will disappear from those regions."

Adolf Hitler (1941)

Definitely not Pentagon material

"I will ignore all ideas for new works and engines of war, the invention of which has reached its limits and for whose improvement I see no further hope."

Julius Frontinus, a Roman military engineer (first century A.D.)

Fission Impossible

"That is the biggest fool thing we have ever done . . . The bomb will never go off, and I speak as an expert in explosives."

U.S. Admiral William D. Leahy to President Truman, on atomic weaponry (1945)

Hanoi-thing you say, Ike

"Whatever happens in Vietnam, I can conceive of nothing except military victory."

Dwight D. Eisenhower (1966)

But duck anyway

"The Nazi threat to unleash U-2 bombs on London is just a meaningless publicity stunt."

> Lord Cherwell, to Winston Churchill
> (1940)

Gee, can't wait till the next war

"In the future, massive floating forts will take the place of our present battleships; these will be able to constantly move their positions, probably under cover of artificial fogs . . . Huge submarines will bring armoured tanks to within, say, a mile of the shores of any country, where they would be disgorged and quickly run to dry land . . . There will naturally be great activity in the air. Huge aeroplanes, launched by compressed air, will convey loads of men and apparatus readily to any point . . ."

> A. M. Low, British journalist, The
> Future (1925)

He never did have a sense of time

"Hitler has missed the bus."

> Prime Minister Neville Chamberlain,
> on the eve of Germany's invasion of
> Norway

6

IT'LL NEVER FLY

Sci-Tech

A dash of skepticism

"I watched his countenance closely, to see if he was not deranged . . . and I was assured by other senators after he left the room that they had no confidence in it."

> U.S. Senator Smith of Indiana, after witnessing a demonstration of Samuel Morses's telegraph (1842)

Dial-a-jerk

"You could put in this room . . . all the radio-telephone apparatus that the country will ever need."

> W. W. Dean, president of the Dean Telephone Company (1907)

Especially if they're in the bar car

"People will not think twice about having to commute 300 or 400 miles to work every day."

> A student report from the Harvard Graduate School of Business Administration, on the implications of nuclear power (1965)

See-through vision

"X-rays are a hoax."

Lord Kelvin, engineer and physicist
(c. 1900)

And the chicken farm ad?

"Don't be surprised if the perfume advertisement in your daily newspaper one day smells fetchingly lovely, while on the next page, the butcher's advertisement gives off a steaky scent mingled with the odor of frying onions."

Dr. Ralph Bienfay, University of Oklahoma (1948)

Must be one of them new, improved flashes

"Television won't last. It's a flash in the pan."

Mary Somerville, radio pioneer (1948)

But then, I've always been pig-headed and close-minded

". . . As far as I can judge, I do not look upon any system of wireless telegraphy as a serious competitor with our cables. Some years ago I said the same thing and nothing has since occurred to alter my views."

Sir John Wolfe-Barry, at a meeting of the stockholders of the Western Telegraph Company (1907)

Do you have anything near-fetched?

". . . too far-fetched to be considered."

> The editor of <u>Scientific American</u>, in a letter to Robert Goddard about Goddard's idea of a rocket-accelerated airplane bomb (1940)

Long-playing blunder

"They never will try to steal the phonograph. It is not of any commercial value."

> Thomas Edison (c. 1915)

Hi-drek

"This extraordinary monument of theoretical genius accordingly remains, and doubtless will for ever remain, a theoretical possibility."

> A biographer of Charles Babbage, inventor of the computer (1883)

Get lost. Stop.

> U.S. Postmaster-General to Samuel Morse, rejecting Morse's offer to sell his telegraph to the government (c. 1844) for $100,000 because

". . . the operation of the telegraph between Washington and Baltimore had not satisfied him that under any rate of postage that could be adopted, its revenues could be made equal to its expenditures."

Patently absurd

"Everything that can be invented has been invented."

U.S. Patent Office Director, urging President McKinley to abolish the office (1899)

Dark day for Tommy

"Everyone acquainted with the subject will recognize it as a conspicuous failure."

Henry Morton, President of The Stevens Institute of Technology, on Edison's incandescent lamp (c. 1880)

I learned that on "Hollywood Squares"

"Television? No good will come of this device. The word is half Greek and half Latin."

C. P. Scott (1846-1932) English jounalist

Dim bulb

"With regard to the electric light, much has been said for and against it, but I think I may say without fear of contradiction that when the Paris Exhibition closes, electric light will close with it, and no more will be heard of it."

Erasmus Wilson, Oxford University professor (1878)

Go get him, R2D2

"There will never be a robot. Even the most ingenious technologist cannot make a collection of wheels, shafts, magnets and wires think."

> Waldemar Kaempffert, American science writer (1927)

Cuts down on those message units, too

"The Americans have need of the telephone, but we do not. We have plenty of messenger boys."

> Sir William Preece, Chief Engineer of the British Post Office (1876)

We can work the kinks out later

"I must confess that my imagination, in spite even of spurring, refuses to see any sort of submarine doing anything but suffocating its crew and floundering at sea."

> H. G. Wells, Anticipations (1901)

Down the tubes

"While theoretically and technically television may be feasible, commercially and financially I consider it an impossibility, a development of which we need waste little time dreaming."

> Lee DeForest, American inventor (1926)

This just in . . .

"Lee DeForest has said in many newspapers and over his signature that it would be possible to transmit the human voice across the Atlantic before many years. Based on these absurd and deliberately misleading statements, the misguided public . . . has been persuaded to purchase stock in his company . . ."

> A U.S. District Attorney, prosecuting American inventor Lee DeForest for selling stock fraudulently through the mail for his Radio Telephone Company (1913)

Whither progress?

"The advancement of the arts from year to year taxes our credulity and seems to presage the arrival of that period when further improvement must end."

> Henry Ellsworth, U.S. Commissioner of Patents, on the future of inventions (1844)

Wonder if they'll have time to study stupid predictions too?

"The amount of misguided ingenuity which has been expended on these two problems of submarine and aerial navigation during the nineteenth century will offer one of the most curious and interesting studies to the future historian of technologic progress."

> George Sutherland, American lawyer, 20th Century Inventions (1900)

Laughing gas

"We thankful are that sun and moon
    Were placed so very high
That no tempestuous hand might reach
    To tear them from the sky.
Were it not so, we soon should find
    That some reforming ass
Would straight propose to snuff them out
    And light the world with Gas."

> Popular rhyme, ridiculing the idea of lighting English cities with gas (early 1800s)

"[They] might as well try to light London with a slice from the moon."

> William H. Wollaston, English chemist and philosopher, addressing the same subject

Neither does my reputation

"Radio has no future."

> Lord Kelvin, engineer and physicist (1904)

We'll leave it for our kids

". . . we need not worry over the consequences of breaking up the atom."

> Floyd Parsons, engineer (1931)

And now, gentlemen, I'm going back to my cave

"I don't believe in aeroplanes, science and progress, in railway timetables or in economic law. I cannot think of them as real, and there will be none of them in my future. There is no room for them. I freely give the lot of them to Messrs. Shaw, Wells, Stalin, Sinclair Lewis, Mussolini and the rest."

Bernard Fay, French philosopher (1933)

Monkey business

". . . I was taught it. It took me more than twenty years of work before I discovered it was wrong."

Douglas Dewar, ornithologist, on evolution

". . . There are . . . absolutely no facts either in the records of geology, or in the history of the past, or in the experience of the present, that can be referred to as proving evolution, or the development of one species from another by selection of any kind whatever."

Louis Agassiz, professor of geology and zoology, Harvard University (1893)

Anyone can have an off century

"The only thing science has done for man in the last hundred years is to create for him fresh moral problems."

The Reverend Geoffrey Fisher, Archbishop of Canterbury (1950)

Melt the butter too?

"The energy available to him [mankind] through the disintegration of radioactive or any other atoms may perhaps be sufficient to keep the corner peanut and popcorn man going on a few street corners in our larger towns for a long time to come, but that is all."

Robert A. Millikan, American physicist (1928)

Always put clothes on your fancies, George

"a web of naked fancies."

A critic's reaction to the publication of physicist George Simon Ohm's theory of electricity (Ohm's law) in 1827

Better run that data through again

"I think there is a world market for about five computers."

Thomas J. Watson, International Business Machines (IBM) (1958)

Other than that, he's a brilliant scholar

"All that was new in them was false and all that was true in them was old."

Professor Haughton, commenting on Charles Darwin's research findings, as published in The Origin of Species

Look for a run on crystal balls

"Everyone sees a new science . . . developed where previously we had not even been conscious that there was a void in our knowledge. In the eighteenth century, it was electricity. In the nineteenth century, psychology. In the twentieth, it is the conviction of the Scientific American that it will be the field to which the rather unsatisfactory name of psychic has been attached."

Scientific American (1920)

Simon says

"I am tired of all this sort of thing called science here . . . We have spent millions in that sort of thing for the last few years, and it is time it should be stopped."

U.S. Senator Simon Cameron, on the Smithsonian Institute (1901)

There's always suicide

"The abolishment of pain in surgery is a chimera. It is absurd to go on seeking it today. 'Knife' and 'pain' are two words in surgery that must forever be associated in the consciousness of the patient. To this compulsory combination we shall have to adjust ourselves."

Dr. Alfred Velpeau, on anesthesia (1839)

Care for a raincheck?

"An increasing number of experts feel that some capability for modifying weather could become feasible during the decade."

National Goals Research Staff report, forecasting for the 1970s (1970)

Shot down

"Cancer, polio, tuberculosis and an array of other sourges will have been consigned to the same limbo as cholera, typhus and other great killers of the past."

David Sarnoff, former chairman of RCA, forecasting for 1980 (1955)

Move over, big fella

"[One hundred years hence] . . . man will be so completely the master of organic law that he would create life in competition with God."

Claude Bernard, French physiologist (1869)

Besides, it's dark in there

"The abdomen, the chest and the brain will be forever shut from the intrusion of the wise and humane surgeon."

Sir John Erichsen, surgeon extraordinary to Queen Victoria, on surgery (1873)

7
BUM CALLS
Sports

I've never been much of a handicapper

"Jackie Robinson won't make the grade this year or ever . . . He's a thousand-to-one shot."

Jimmy Power, sports editor, New York Daily News (1947)

How 'bout shipping a load of manure to the Bronx?

"I won't be involved in the day-by-day operations of the team. I'm too busy with the shipping business."

George Steinbrenner, Yankees owner (1973)

Anyone for an eggshell?

"Champion of the world my eye. That kid ain't got the guts to fill a thimble."

Jerry Lisker, New York Post, quoting his own appraisal in the early '60s of the boxing future of a youngster named Cassius Clay (a/k/a Muhammad Ali)

Pete Rozelle told us so

"Baseball is a beat-up, dying sport."

Forbes magazine (1971)

Gee, imagine if he were a young thirty

"He's an old thirty."

Bill DeWitt, Cincinnati Red owner on why he traded Frank Robinson (1966)

Anyone for slim?

"Playing the Russians will be a lesson in futility. You defense them one way, they come at you another way. You know what our chances are? Slim and none."

Herb Brooks, coach of the 1980 U.S. Olympic hockey team

If only the body was as willing as the mouth

"I'm gonna beat up on him so bad it'll be a total mismatch."

Muhammad Ali, before being humiliated by Larry Holmes

Right up there with Bill Hosket

"He's gonna be a helluva pro."

Red Auerbach, on the future of college star Neal Walk (1969)

Come here and say that, wimp

"The growing gentleness of mankind will abolish, as barbarous, games which take the form of modified assault, as football, boxing, wrestling, fencing and the like."

T. Baron Russell, A Hundred Years Hence (1905)

Speaking of grave mistakes

"Ruth made a grave mistake. Working once a week, he might have lasted a long time and become a great star."

Baseball great Tris Speaker, on Babe Ruth's decision to forsake pitching to become an everyday player (c. 1920)

(Scrambled) Egg on the face

"The kid will never last more than two or three years."

Gino Marchetti, defensive end for the Baltimore Colts, on scrambling rookie quarterback Fran Tarkenton (1961)

And when that doesn't work, we steal it

"I like to use that line from the TV commercial: 'We make our money the old-fashioned way: we earn it.'"

Harold "Ross Fields" Smith, former boxing promoter convicted of embezzling $21.3 million from a bank

Then, again, how could I do worse?

"As soon as I get a chance to dedicate myself to baseball, I think I'll do better."

> Danny Ainge, pro basketball player before deciding to abandon his career as a major league infielder (1981)

Why the Chicago Cubs haven't won a pennant since 1945

"He won't make it."

> Cub scout Gordon Goldsberry, on the professional prospects for a young pitcher named Tom Seaver (c. 1966)

In the dark

"Just a fad. A passing fancy."

> Philip Wrigley, longtime owner of baseball's Chicago Cubs, on playing games at night (c. 1935)

Look homeward, Angel

". . . I'll be here the rest of my life. I'll always be identified with Oakland, and Oakland with me."

> Slugger Reggie Jackson (1973)

But he makes a good cup of coffee

"You just bought yourself a cripple."

> Pittsburgh Pirates manager Bill Terry, to New York Yankees general manager George Weiss, after the Yanks surrendered five players and $25,000 for the rights to a young player named Joe DiMaggio, who had a knee injury (1936)

Scratch a rising star

"You'll never make it in this league."

> New York Yankees owner George Steinbrenner, to pitcher Ron Guidry, after a poor Guidry outing (1976)

I'll never figure why people think I'm spoiled

"Football doesn't pay much."

> Johann Cruyff, Dutch soccer star and reputed millionaire (1973)

Gee, who should we root for?

"It will probably be the great sport event in history. Bigger than the Frazier-Ali fight. It really is the free world against the lying, cheating, hypocritical Russians."

> Bobby Fischer, on his world chess championship match against Boris Spassky (1972)

Other than that, he's champion material

"Rocky Marciano can't fight a lick, his footwork is what you'd expect from two left feet, he throws his right in a clumsy circle and knows nothing of orderly retreat. All he can do is blast the breath from your lungs or knock your head off."

> Anonymous boxing writer, on Rocky Marciano

That's about right

"I bought this team for $100,000, and I'd say that in a few years it could be worth four or five million. . . Nothing has the financial potential of women's basketball."

> Larry Kozlicki, owner of the Nebraska Wranglers, of the defunct Women's Basketball League (1979)

Four eyes scores again

"He's too awkward. Besides, he wears glasses."

> George Koegan, Notre Dame basketball coach, on why he didn't recruit George Mikan

Le Gaffe

"Reggie Jackson will play in Montreal."

> Charles Bronfman, chairman of the Montreal Expos (1976)

There's no fooling football players

> "The first thing I said when I came on this campus is that before you can start winning, you have to stop losing."

> > Iowa football coach Hayden Fry (1981)

Sounds like surefire Hall-of-Fame material

> "Don't do it. He's not ready. I've seen a sandlot team clobber him. All he'll do is take up space for two years and give the papers more ammunition to throw at you."

> > Branch Rickey, Jr., of the Dodgers, to his father, who was the team's general manager, urging him not to sign a young pitching prospect named Sandy Koufax

Anyone for paternity leave?

> "The Olympic Games can no more have a deficit than a man can have a baby."

> > Jean Drapeau, mayor of Montreal, shortly before the opening of the 1976 Olympic Games

And as long as we're making predictions, I'll never be in another fight either

> "I'll never go back to the Yankees."

> > Billy Martin (March 1982)

But in which direction?

"He's going to turn whatever pro team gets him right around—just the way Lew Alcindor did at Milwaukee."

> Lucius Mitchell, Kentucky State basketball coach, on his star center, Elmore Smith

Give the man a shovel

"We will bury you."

> Soviet track official to his U.S. counterpart, prior to 1964 U.S.-U.S.S.R. meet in which the U.S. won 16 of the 22 events

Nice detail, though

"Holmes will come out in the first round, showing a great deal of disdain and will immediately try for a quick knockout. This will be his downfall. Cooney, big and strong but not to be regarded as a Primo Carnera or that other giant, Abe Simon, will show us he's a fighter when in the very first round he will hook a left to the body, followed by a left upstairs and then a right. Two lefts and the right and it will all be over. Cooney by knockout in the first round."

> Art Rust, Jr., boxing authority and sports show host, on the Larry Holmes-Gerry Cooney fight (June 1982)

What, me biased?

"Isn't it obvious by now? The Dodgers are a fine team, a gutsy team, the best team in the National League. But they can't beat the Yankees because the Yankees are a better baseball team."

New York Post sportwriter Henry Hecht, just prior to the Dodgers' taking four straight over the Yankees to win the 1981 World Series

8
FOLLIES
The Arts

Yeah, yeah, yeah

"The Beatles are just a passing phase. They are a sign of the uncertainties of the times."

The Reverend Billy Graham (1964)

Then, again, he thinks my philosophy is upchuck

"Is Wagner a human being at all? He contaminates everything he touches—he has made music sick. I postulate this viewpoint: Wagner's art is diseased."

Friedrich Nietzsche (1844-1900), German philosopher

Besides, albums are really getting expensive

"The effect of rock and roll on young people is to turn them into devil worshipers, to stimulate self-expression through sex, to provoke lawlessness, impair nervous stability and destroy the sanctity of marriage. It is an evil influence on the youth of our country."

The Reverend Albert Carter, pentacostal minister

If this doesn't bring back "Charlie's Angels," nothing will

"Three-dimensional color television, with smell, touch, and taste added, may be available by the 1990s."

> Desmond King-Hele, scientist and mathematician

Take "The Dukes of Hazzard," for instance

". . . Television drama of high caliber and produced by first-rate artists will materially raise the level of dramatic taste of the nation, just as aural broadcasting has raised the level of musical appreciation."

> David Sarnoff, former chairman of RCA (c. 1955)

See you at the Pink Pussycat Cinema

"Every one of the fine arts will be more generally and more subtly appreciated than now."

> T. Baron Russell, <u>A Hundred Years Hence</u>, forecasting events in the 20th century (1905)

I can pick out a born secretary anywhere

"You'd better learn secretarial work or else get married."

> Emmeline Snively, head of Blue Book Modeling Agency, to Marilyn Monroe (1944)

Jesus goes the way of the hula hoop

"Christianity will go. It will vanish and shrink. I needn't argue about that. I'm right and will be proved right. We're more popular than Jesus now."

John Lennon, member of The Beatles (1966)

Gooney tunes

"Rock 'n' roll is phony and false, and sung, written and played for the most part by cretinous goons."

Frank Sinatra (1957)

Discomfort bags provided for your convenience

". . . I would like to know of what this Institution consists. I would like the gentleman from New York [Mr. Pruyn] or the gentleman from Vermont [Mr. Poland] to tell us how many of his constituents ever saw this Institution or ever will see it or ever want to see it? It is enough to make any man or woman sick to visit that Institution . . ."

U.S. Congressman Lewis Selye, reacting to an appropriations bill for the Smithsonian Institute (1869)

Et tu, Walt?

"Shakespeare's comedies are altogether non-acceptable to America or Democracy."

Walt Whitman (1819-92), American poet

Multitalented

"Can't act. Can't sing. Slightly bald. Can dance a little."

> Studio talent scout, after viewing
> Fred Astaire's first screen test

He's just bitter 'cause he couldn't get Stones tickets

"If we cannot stem the tide of rock 'n' roll with its waves of rhythmic narcosis and of future waves of vicarious craze, we are preparing our own downfall in the midst of pandemonic funeral dances."

> A. M. Meerio, associate professor of psychiatry, Columbia University (1957)

Hey, there's more to flinging than you think

"I have seen and heard much of Cockney impudence before now; but never expected to hear a coxcomb ask two hundred guineas for flinging a pot of paint in the public's face."

> John Ruskin, English art critic and social reformer, after viewing Whistler exhibition (1878)

It can't hurt to look

"You'll never find anyone to sing those songs."

> Actress Anne Bancroft to Broadway producers Bob Merrill and Jules Styne, after hearing the score of Funny Girl

9

ERRORTICA

Life Between the Sexes

Bed 'n bored

"By 1975 sexual feeling and marriage will have nothing to do with each other."

John Langdon-Davies, <u>A Short History of the Future</u> (1936)

Particularly when your partner's parents walk in on you

"Premarital sex can be a source of severe psychic disturbances and can lead to social impoverishment of the personality."

An unidentified Soviet professor

And if that doesn't work, try lacy underwear

"White sugar is the curse of civilization—it causes fatigue and sexual apathy between husband and wife. My recipe against sexual fatigue is to take honey in large quantities; two Gev-E-Tabs, ten vitamin E pills, four wheatgerm oil tablets, four vitamin A pills, four bonemeal tablets, six liver-plus tablets, two dessert-spoons of Bio-Strath Elixir, twice a day."

Barbara Cartland, English romance novelist

It's right here in the latest Hustler

"Women resist in order to be conquered."

Octavio Piccolomini (1599-1656),
Italian general

Taking the mystery out of childbirth

"If it is a male [the fetus], the right breast swells first, the right eye is brighter than the left, the face is high-colored, because the color is such as the blood is, and as the male is conceived of purer blood and of more perfect seed than the female."

Aristotle

Sperm warfare

"The essential thing for the future is to have lots of children. Everybody should be persuaded that the family's life is assured only when it has upwards of four children—I should even say, four sons."

Adolf Hitler (1941)

The Power of Paternal Thinking

"And, if in act of copulation, the woman earnestly look on the man, and fix her mind on him, the child will resemble its father. Nay, if a woman, even in unlawful copulation, fix her mind upon her husband, the child will resemble him though he did not beget it."

Aristotle (4th century B.C.)

And men will love them for their minds

"Women will propose marriage."

> L. N. Boyd, editor of The Fairmont (West Virginia) Gazette, looking ahead one hundred years (1867)

Keep your mind on the sermon, fellas

". . . it would be impossible for the male members of the average Anglican congregation to be present at a service at which a woman ministered without becoming unduly conscious of her sex."

> Commission appointed by the Archbishop of Canterbury (1935)

Hands off

"If practiced in girlhood, does it affect married life? Yes, those girls who practice it fail to develop as women. They become flat-chested and lose the female glow which draws gentlemen around them."

> Orson Squire Fowler, on female masturbation (1870)

It's all downhill after puberty

"All well-sexed maidens enter womanhood with a plump, luscious bust, which usually shrivels gradually till it almost disappears by age twenty."

> Orson Squire Fowler, Sexual Science (1870)

End of an ERA

"The women's liberation movement will expire."

William F. Buckley, author and pub-
lisher, offering a prediction about
the '80s (1980)

So much for the singles scene

"Though marriage has many pains, celibacy has no pleasures.
The unmarried are outlaws of human nature. They are
peevish at home and malevolent abroad. They dream away
their time without friendship or fondness and are driven by
boredom to childish amusements or vicious delights. To live
without feeling or exciting sympathy, to be fortunate without
adding to the felicity of others . . . is a state more gloomy than
solitude: it is not retreat but exclusion from mankind."

Samuel Johnson (1709-84) English
writer

I'd love to, hon, but I had pigeon tonight

"Wood pigeons check and blunt the manly powers; let him not eat
this bird who wishes to be amorous."

Martial (c. 40-104 A.D.), Roman poet

10
FUTURE SCHLOCK
The World of Tomorrow

Today's impertinence

"Violence breeds violence, and it is predicted that by 1990 kidnapping will be the dominant mode of social interaction."

Woody Allen, American playwright and actor (1982)

Other than that, it should be a picnic

"In a hundred years, there will be no literary tastes and no literature. A mob of machine drivers will rule. Every hour will be lived by mankind in talk, nothing but talk. There will be no silence, no retirement, no village life. A gaping crowd of conceited fools will be everywhere. There will be no calm, contented days, no beautiful nights, no good works. All will be the same, all common. Thought and inspiration will be dead."

T. F. Powys, English author (c. 1930)

But we'll die trying, won't we?

"You can never plan the future from the past."

Edmund Burke, (1729-97). British political thinker

Don't you think that's a mite quixotic?

"There will be no C, X or Q in our everyday alphabet. They will be abandoned because unnecessary."

John Elfreth Watkins, Jr., American journalist, predicting for the year 2001 (1900)

Where'd we go wrong, Willy?

"It is not necessary to look too far into the future; we see enough already to be certain that it will be magnificent."

Wilbur Wright (1908)

Requiem for Mickey and Willard

"Rats and mice will have been exterminated."

John Elfreth Watkins, Jr., American journalist, predicting for the year 2001 (1900)

Ms.-ing the boat

". . . Young women live within an enclave where even in the year 2000, it may be more damaging to be thought homely or lacking in sex appeal than to be stupid. Their standing will still depend at least as much on the men to whom they attach themselves as on their own achievements in meritocratic terms."

David Riesman, American social scientist, Harvard University (1965)

Casting a poll on foretelling

"It makes no sense to predict the future. There are too many contingencies."

George Gallup, American pollster

Pull up a chair

"Do you know that in three or four hundred years all the earth will become a flourishing garden? And life will then be exceedingly easy and comfortable?"

Anton Chekhov (1860-1904), Russian writer

I much prefer predicting the past

"Prediction is very difficult, especially about the future."

Niels Bohr, Danish scientist

Just another Pollyanna

"It is now more than probable that our science, our civilization, our great and real advance in the practice of government are only bringing us nearer to the day when the lower races will predominate the world, when the high races will lose their noblest elements, when we shall ask nothing from the day but to live, nor from the future but that we may not deteriorate."

Charles Pearson, writer

Another few eons and we should be in great shape

"Nature has set no bounds on the improvement of human faculties . . . the perfectability of man is really indefinite . . ."

> Marquis de Condorcet, French philosopher (c. 1785)

Mein kid

"A minister from the Northeast will admit that he is Adolf Hitler's love child."

> Clarissa Bernhardt, psychic (1982)

They'll love Lucy

"Lucille Ball will become ambassador to an Asian country."

> Daniel Logan, psychic, making a prediction for 1979-80

And then turn it over to David Brenner for a month

"Johnny Carson will rent the space shuttle and will host the first-ever television show from space."

> Clarissa Berhardt, psychic (1982)

Mother Nature on the bread line

"When we have ascertained, by means of science, the method of Nature's operations, we shall be able to take her place and to perform them for ourselves. When we understand the laws which regulate the complex phenomena of life we shall be able to predict the future as we are already able to predict comets and eclipses and the planetary movements."

Winwood Reade, British writer and thinker, from The Martydom of Man (1872)

EPILOGUE

Now he tells us

"Cease to inquire what the future has in store, and take as a gift whatever the day brings forth."

>Horace (65-8 B.C.), Roman philosopher

I knew you were going to say that

"You can predict things only after they've happened."

>Eugene Ionesco (1912-   ), French playwright